1

<u>Table of Contents</u>

Preface:

In a world inundated with the allure of Singing Songs music, dance, and related entertainment, the teachings of Islam stand as a beacon of guidance, illuminating the path towards spiritual purity and righteousness. "The Essence of Tawheed and Taqwa: Protecting Against the Pitfalls of Musical singing Songs and dance Temptation" delves into the fundamental concepts of Tawheed (the Oneness of Allah) and Taqwa (God-consciousness), offering invaluable insights into their significance in the context of resisting the temptations of music and dance.

As believers striving to navigate the complexities of contemporary society, it becomes imperative to understand the detrimental effects of succumbing to the seductive melodies and rhythms that permeate our surroundings. This book serves as a comprehensive guide, shedding light on the spiritual, moral, and societal ramifications of indulging in musical and dance-related activities contrary to Islamic principles.

Through a series of thought-provoking questions and answers, readers are invited to embark on a journey of self-reflection and introspection, exploring the profound wisdom embedded within the teachings of Islam. From the importance of Tawheed in shaping our worldview to the practical steps one can take to cultivate Taqwa in daily life, each chapter offers invaluable guidance for navigating the challenges posed by musical temptation.

Drawing upon the wisdom of the Quran, Sunnah, and scholarly insights, this book equips readers with the knowledge and understanding needed to safeguard their souls against the whispers of Shaytan and the allure of worldly pleasures. It emphasizes the transformative power of Tawheed and Taqwa in fostering spiritual resilience, moral integrity, and unwavering devotion to the pleasure of Allah.

As we embark on this journey together, let us heed the call to prioritize our commitment to Tawheed and Taqwa, recognizing them as our steadfast companions in the pursuit of spiritual excellence and divine favor. May this book serve as a source of enlightenment and inspiration, guiding us towards a life imbued with piety, righteousness, and unwavering faith in the Oneness of Allah.

"The Essence of Tawheed and Taqwa: Protecting Against the Pitfalls of Musical Temptation"

What is Tawheed and why is it important in Islam?

Tawheed is the belief in the Oneness of Allah and is fundamental to Islam as it defines the monotheistic nature of the faith.

How does understanding Tawheed help in resisting musical temptation?

Understanding Tawheed strengthens our faith in Allah, making us more conscious of His commands and less susceptible to worldly distractions.

What role does Taqwa play in protecting against sins like music and dance?

Taqwa, or God-consciousness, acts as a shield against sins by instilling a fear of displeasing Allah and a desire to adhere to His guidance.

How can one develop Taqwa in their daily life?

Developing Taqwa involves increasing awareness of Allah's presence, striving to follow His commands, and seeking His forgiveness for any shortcomings.

Why is music often considered harmful in Islam?

Music is considered harmful because it can lead to distractions from worship, promote sinful behavior, and foster a love for worldly pleasures over spiritual growth.

What are some of the consequences of indulging in music and dance?

Indulging in music and dance can lead to spiritual degradation, moral corruption, and distance from the teachings of Islam.

How does Tawheed guide us in making choices regarding music and entertainment?

Tawheed reminds us of our ultimate purpose in life—to worship Allah alone—and encourages us to align our actions with His pleasure.

What are some practical steps one can take to avoid the temptation of music and dance?

Practical steps include seeking halal alternatives for entertainment, surrounding oneself with like-minded individuals, and increasing engagement in beneficial activities such as Quran recitation and dhikr.

How can parents and educators instill the importance of Tawheed and Taqwa in children and youth?

Parents and educators can lead by example, provide religious education, and create environments conducive to spiritual growth.

What are the spiritual benefits of prioritizing Tawheed and Taqwa over worldly pleasures?

Prioritizing Tawheed and Taqwa brings inner peace, contentment, and closeness to Allah, leading to a more fulfilling and purposeful life.

How does understanding the concept of accountability in Islam relate to Tawheed and Taqwa?

Understanding accountability reminds us of our responsibility to Allah and motivates us to live in accordance with His guidance out of fear and hope in His mercy.

What advice does Islam offer for those struggling to resist the temptations of music and dance?

Islam advises seeking help through prayer, seeking forgiveness for past mistakes, and seeking support from knowledgeable individuals and community resources.

How can the Quran and Sunnah serve as guides for understanding and implementing Tawheed and Taqwa?

The Quran and Sunnah provide clear guidance on the importance of Tawheed and Taqwa and offer practical examples of how to live a righteous life.

What role does self-reflection and introspection play in strengthening one's commitment to Tawheed and Taqwa?

Self-reflection and introspection help individuals identify areas for improvement, acknowledge their weaknesses, and strive for spiritual growth.

How does gratitude and remembrance of Allah contribute to the cultivation of Tawheed and Taqwa?

Gratitude and remembrance of Allah foster a deeper connection to Him and reinforce the importance of prioritizing His pleasure above all else.

What are some common misconceptions about Tawheed and Taqwa, particularly regarding music and entertainment?

Common misconceptions include viewing Tawheed and Taqwa as restrictive rather than liberating, and perceiving music and entertainment as harmless forms of recreation.

How can communities promote a culture of Tawheed and Taqwa, especially among youth?

Communities can promote Tawheed and Taqwa by organizing educational programs, fostering supportive environments, and providing outlets for halal recreation.

What role do Islamic scholars and leaders play in guiding believers towards Tawheed and Taqwa in the context of music and dance?

Islamic scholars and leaders provide valuable insights and guidance based on Islamic principles, helping believers navigate complex issues and make informed decisions.

How can the teachings of Islam regarding Tawheed and Taqwa be applied in everyday life, including social interactions and entertainment choices?

The teachings of Islam can be applied by prioritizing obedience to Allah in all aspects of life, including social interactions, entertainment choices, and personal conduct.

What are the long-term benefits of embracing Tawheed and Taqwa, particularly in the face of societal pressures and temptations?

Embracing Tawheed and Taqwa leads to spiritual fulfillment, moral integrity, and eternal reward, providing believers with strength and resilience to overcome worldly challenges.

For more information visit Quranexplains.com or contact Sheikh Touqeer Ansari.

Understanding the Prohibition of Music in Islam: Guidance for Teenagers

Q: Why is music considered forbidden in Islam?

A: Music is considered haram in Islam because it can lead to distractions from worship and devotional activities, as well as promote immoral behavior such as dancing or attending venues like casinos.

Q: What are some examples of activities where music is commonly used but is prohibited in Islam?

A: Music is often used in activities like dancing, attending football games, or playing games that require music before they start, all of which are discouraged in Islam.

Q: How does listening to music affect our spirituality and focus on worship?

A: Listening to music can divert our attention away from Allah and hinder our ability to focus on prayer and other religious obligations.

Q: Why is it important for teenagers to understand the prohibition of music in Islam?

A: It's important for teenagers to understand so they can make informed choices that align with Islamic principles and avoid engaging in activities that may lead them away from the teachings of Islam.

Q: How can teenagers resist peer pressure to engage in activities involving music?

A: Teenagers can resist peer pressure by staying firm in their beliefs, surrounding themselves with like-minded friends, and finding alternative activities that are in accordance with Islamic teachings.

Q: What are the spiritual dangers of indulging in music-related activities?

A: Indulging in music-related activities can weaken one's spirituality, lead to a decrease in religious commitment, and distance individuals from their faith.

Q: How can teenagers channel their energy and creativity into halal (permissible) activities?

A: Teenagers can channel their energy and creativity into activities such as sports, arts, volunteering, and learning about Islam, which are encouraged and permissible in Islam.

Q: What are some alternative forms of entertainment that align with Islamic principles?

A: Alternative forms of entertainment include reading beneficial books, spending time with family and friends, engaging in outdoor activities, and participating in community service.

Q: How does the prohibition of music contribute to maintaining a wholesome and righteous society?

A: The prohibition of music helps promote a society based on morality, righteousness, and devotion to Allah, fostering an environment conducive to spiritual growth and well-being.

Q: What role do parents and mentors play in guiding teenagers away from music-related activities?

A: Parents and mentors play a crucial role in educating teenagers about the harms of music and providing guidance and support to help them make virtuous choices.

Q: How can teenagers educate themselves about the Islamic perspective on music?

A: Teenagers can educate themselves by studying Islamic texts, attending lectures or seminars on Islamic ethics, and seeking guidance from knowledgeable scholars and elders.

Q: What are some practical steps teenagers can take to avoid music-related activities?

A: Practical steps include avoiding environments where music is prevalent, politely declining invitations to events involving music, and finding halal alternatives for entertainment.

Q: How does understanding the wisdom behind the prohibition of music strengthen teenagers' faith?

A: Understanding the wisdom behind the prohibition reinforces teenagers' faith by helping them recognize the importance of obedience to Allah's commands and the preservation of spiritual purity.

Q: How can teenagers explain the Islamic stance on music to their peers?

A: Teenagers can explain by sharing knowledge about the harmful effects of music on spirituality and encouraging their peers to consider alternative forms of entertainment that are in line with Islamic values.

Q: What are the long-term consequences of indulging in music-related activities?

A: Indulging in music-related activities can have long-term consequences such as desensitization to sin, spiritual distancing from Allah, and difficulty in breaking away from harmful habits.

Q: How can teenagers contribute to creating a more spiritually aware and righteous community?

A: Teenagers can contribute by setting a positive example, promoting Islamic values among their peers, and actively participating in initiatives that promote spiritual growth and moral integrity.

Q: How does adherence to Islamic teachings regarding music lead to personal growth and self-discipline?

A: Adherence to Islamic teachings fosters personal growth and self-discipline by instilling a sense of responsibility, self-control, and commitment to living a life that pleases Allah.

Q: What guidance does Islam provide for teenagers seeking fulfillment and joy without music?

A: Islam provides guidance by encouraging teenagers to seek fulfillment and joy through acts of worship, service to others, cultivating positive relationships, and engaging in wholesome activities that nurture the soul.

Q: How can teenagers find strength and resilience in their faith when faced with societal pressures regarding music?

A: Teenagers can find strength and resilience in their faith by deepening their connection with Allah through prayer, seeking support from fellow believers, and remaining steadfast in their commitment to Islamic principles.

Exploring Islam: Understanding Why Music is Forbidden

Q: Can we listen to music in Islam?

A: No, dear, in Islam, we don't listen to music because it can lead us to do things that are not good.

Q: Why is music not allowed in Islam?

A: Music is not allowed because it might make us do things that are against what Allah wants for us.

Q: What are some things we might do if we listen to music?

A: We might want to dance or play games that are not good for us if we listen to music.

Q: Does playing video games with music count as listening to music?

A: Yes, playing video games with music is like listening to music, so it's better for us not to do it.

Q: Can we play games that have music before they start?

A: No, we should avoid playing games that have music in them because it can make us forget about Allah.

Q: Why does Allah not want us to listen to music?

A: Allah wants us to do things that are good for us and make us better people. Music can sometimes make us do things that are not good.

Q: What can we do instead of listening to music?

A: We can do many fun things like playing outside, reading books, or spending time with our family and friends.

Q: Can we still have fun without music?

A: Yes, we can have lots of fun without music! There are so many other things we can do that make us happy.

Q: What does it mean for something to be "haram"?

A: Haram means something is not allowed in Islam because it can lead us away from Allah and doing good things.

Q: Should we listen to what Allah says even if we want to listen to music?

A: Yes, we should always listen to what Allah says because He knows what is best for us.

Q: How can we remember not to listen to music?

A: We can remind ourselves by thinking about Allah and remembering that He wants us to do what is right.

Q: Can we listen to music if it's for a school project or a special occasion?

A: It's better not to listen to music even for school projects or special occasions because there are always other ways to do things.

Q: What can we do if our friends want to listen to music?

A: We can politely tell them that we don't listen to music because it's against what we believe in Islam.

Q: Can music distract us from remembering Allah?

A: Yes, music can sometimes distract us from remembering Allah and doing good things.

Q: What are some good things we can do instead of listening to music?

A: We can pray, read Quran, help others, and learn new things about Islam.

Q: How can we explain to our friends why we don't listen to music?

A: We can tell them that listening to music is against what we believe in Islam and that we want to do what is right.

Q: Does everyone in Islam agree that music is not allowed?

A: Most Muslims believe that music is not allowed, but some people might have different opinions.

Q: Can we ask our parents or teachers about why music is not allowed in Islam?

A: Yes, we can always ask our parents or teachers about Islam, and they will help us understand.

Q: What does Allah want us to do instead of listening to music?

A: Allah wants us to do things that make us better people and bring us closer to Him, like praying and being kind to others.

Q: Can we still have fun and be happy without listening to music?

A: Yes, we can have lots of fun and be very happy without listening to music! There are so many wonderful things in life to enjoy.

For more information visit Quranexplains.com or contact Sheikh Touqeer Ansari.

"Understanding the Prohibition of Music in Islam: Consequences and Considerations"

Q: Why is music considered haram (forbidden) in Islam?

A: Music is considered haram because it can lead us to engage in activities that are harmful to ourselves and others, and it can distract us from remembering Allah.

Q: Can music addiction be harmful to our health?

A: Yes, just like any addiction, music addiction can have negative effects on our mental and emotional well-being. It can lead to conditions such as anxiety, depression, and even brain disorders.

Q: How can music distract us from remembering Allah?

A: Music can consume our thoughts and attention, making it difficult for us to focus on our prayers, Quranic recitation, or other acts of worship.

Q: Can music lead to harmful behaviors?

A: Yes, music can sometimes promote harmful behaviors such as substance abuse, promiscuity, and violence.

Q: Are there any scientific studies that show the negative effects of music on the brain?

A: Yes, studies have shown that excessive exposure to certain types of music can lead to changes in brain chemistry and structure, contributing to addiction and other mental health issues.

Q: Can playing video games with music have similar effects?

A: Yes, playing video games with music can also be addictive and lead to similar negative effects on mental health and behavior.

Q: How can we protect ourselves from the negative influence of music?

A: We can protect ourselves by avoiding listening to music altogether and surrounding ourselves with positive influences that align with Islamic teachings.

Q: What are some alternative activities we can engage in instead of listening to music?

A: We can engage in activities such as reading Quran, spending time with family, volunteering, and pursuing hobbies that are productive and beneficial.

Q: Can music have an impact on our relationships with others?

A: Yes, music with inappropriate lyrics or themes can negatively influence our relationships with family and friends, leading to conflicts or misunderstandings.

Q: How does Islam promote moderation in all aspects of life, including entertainment?

A: Islam encourages us to maintain balance and moderation in all aspects of our lives, including our entertainment choices, to avoid harmful excesses.

Q: Can music affect our emotions and mood?
A: Yes, music has the power to influence our emotions and mood, sometimes leading to negative feelings or behaviors.

Q: Are there any exceptions to the prohibition of music in Islam?

A: Some scholars permit certain types of music for educational or religious purposes, such as Islamic nasheeds or classical music without inappropriate lyrics.

Q: How can we resist peer pressure to listen to music?

A: We can strengthen our resolve by reminding ourselves of the negative consequences of listening to music and seeking support from like-minded friends and family members.

Q: Can music contribute to societal problems such as substance abuse and violence?

A: Yes, music that glorifies substance abuse, violence, or other harmful behaviors can contribute to societal problems by influencing listeners' attitudes and behaviors.

Q: Does Islam provide guidance on choosing appropriate forms of entertainment?

A: Yes, Islam encourages us to seek entertainment that is wholesome, uplifting, and in accordance with Islamic values.

Q: How can parents and educators help children understand the dangers of music addiction?

A: Parents and educators can educate children about the harmful effects of music addiction and provide alternative forms of entertainment and recreation.

Q: Can music consumption interfere with our spiritual growth and development?

A: Yes, excessive music consumption can distract us from our spiritual goals and hinder our progress in seeking closeness to Allah.

Q: What role does self-discipline play in resisting the temptation to listen to music?

A: Self-discipline is essential in adhering to Islamic teachings and resisting the temptation to engage in activities that are prohibited or harmful.

Q: How can we use our time and energy more productively instead of listening to music?

A: We can use our time and energy to engage in activities that contribute to our personal growth, education, and spiritual well-being.

Q: What are some Quranic verses and hadiths that emphasize the importance of avoiding harmful influences?

A: Quranic verses and hadiths emphasize the importance of guarding our hearts and minds against harmful influences and seeking Allah's protection from temptation and sin.

For more information visit Quranexplains.com or contact Sheikh Touqeer Ansari.

"Navigating Teenage Challenges: Understanding the Consequences of Music in Islam"

Q: Why is music considered haram (forbidden) in Islam?

A: Music is considered haram because it can lead us away from the remembrance of Allah and towards harmful behaviors.

Q: Can music influence our thoughts and actions?

A: Yes, music has the power to influence our thoughts, emotions, and behaviors, sometimes leading us towards activities that are displeasing to Allah.

Q: What are some negative consequences of listening to music?

A: Listening to music can distract us from our obligations to Allah, lead to addiction, and contribute to negative behaviors such as substance abuse and promiscuity.

Q: How can music affect our mental health?

A: Excessive exposure to music, especially music with inappropriate lyrics or themes, can contribute to anxiety, depression, and other mental health issues.

Q: Can music impact our relationships with family and friends?

A: Yes, music with inappropriate content can lead to conflicts with family members and friends who may have different values or beliefs.

Q: Are there any physical health risks associated with listening to music?

A: Yes, listening to music at high volumes for prolonged periods can damage hearing and contribute to other health issues such as headaches and stress.

Q: How does music consumption affect our spirituality?

A: Music consumption can distract us from our spiritual growth and development by occupying our time and attention with worldly pursuits.

Q: Can music addiction lead to other harmful behaviors?

A: Yes, music addiction can sometimes serve as a gateway to other addictive behaviors, such as substance abuse or excessive screen time.

Q: How can teenagers find alternative forms of entertainment without music?

A: Teenagers can explore activities such as sports, art, volunteering, and spending quality time with family and friends as alternatives to listening to music.

Q: What role does self-discipline play in avoiding music consumption?

A: Self-discipline is essential in resisting the temptation to listen to music and adhering to Islamic teachings even in the face of peer pressure.

Q: Can music consumption affect our academic performance?

A: Yes, excessive music consumption can distract us from studying and other academic responsibilities, leading to lower grades and academic difficulties.

Q: How can teenagers educate themselves about the negative effects of music?

A: Teenagers can research and learn about the harmful effects of music through Islamic teachings, scientific studies, and personal experiences of others.

Q: What steps can teenagers take to resist peer pressure related to music?

A: Teenagers can surround themselves with friends who share similar values, communicate assertively about their beliefs, and seek support from trusted adults.

Q: How can parents and educators support teenagers in resisting music consumption?

A: Parents and educators can provide guidance, set clear expectations, and create a supportive environment that reinforces Islamic values and beliefs.

Q: Are there any Islamic teachings that emphasize the importance of avoiding harmful influences?

A: Yes, Islamic teachings emphasize the importance of guarding our hearts and minds against harmful influences and seeking Allah's protection from temptation and sin.

Q: Can music consumption affect our emotional well-being?

A: Yes, music consumption can influence our emotions, sometimes leading to feelings of sadness, anger, or dissatisfaction.

Q: How can teenagers use their time and energy more productively?

A: Teenagers can engage in activities that contribute to personal growth, education, and spiritual development, such as reading Quran, volunteering, and pursuing hobbies.

Q: Can music consumption interfere with our sleep patterns?

A: Yes, listening to music late at night or before bed can disrupt sleep patterns and contribute to insomnia or other sleep-related issues.

Q: What are some strategies for managing cravings or urges to listen to music?

A: Teenagers can distract themselves with alternative activities, seek support from friends or family, and remind themselves of the negative consequences of music consumption.

Q: How can teenagers cultivate a stronger connection with Allah to resist the influence of music?

A: Teenagers can strengthen their faith through regular prayer, Quranic recitation, and seeking knowledge about Islam, which can help them resist temptations and make choices that align with their beliefs and values.

For more information visit Quranexplains.com or contact Sheikh Touqeer Ansari.

"The Transformative Power of Listening to the Quran: Benefits, Blessings, and Guidance"

Q: What are the benefits of listening to the Quran instead of music?

A: Listening to the Quran can bring peace to the heart, increase faith, and provide spiritual nourishment unlike music which can lead to distractions and worldly desires.

Q: How does listening to the Quran help in building Tawheed (belief in the Oneness of Allah)?

A: Listening to the Quran reinforces the belief in the Oneness of Allah by reminding us of His majesty, power, and mercy as revealed in His words.

Q: What is Taqwa, and how does listening to the Quran help in cultivating it?

A: Taqwa is the consciousness of Allah and the fear of disobeying Him. Listening to the Quran instills Taqwa by reminding us of our duties towards Allah and His guidance for righteous living.

Q: How do we differentiate between music and Quranic recitations?

A: Music often contains lyrics or beats that may promote worldly desires, while Quranic recitations are characterized by their purity, spirituality, and adherence to Islamic principles.

Q: What are some tangible benefits of regularly listening to different reciters of the Quran?

A: Regularly listening to different reciters of the Quran helps improve memorization, enhances understanding of Arabic language, and deepens spiritual connection with the Quran.

Q: How does listening to the Quran contribute to emotional well-being?

A: Listening to the Quran can soothe the heart, alleviate stress and anxiety, and provide solace during difficult times, unlike music which may temporarily distract but not provide lasting peace.

Q: Can listening to the Quran have positive effects on physical health?

A: Yes, studies have shown that listening to the Quran can reduce blood pressure, lower stress levels, and promote overall well-being, unlike music which may not have the same holistic benefits.

Q: How does the Quran serve as a source of guidance for various aspects of life?

A: The Quran offers guidance on matters of faith, morality, ethics, relationships, governance, and more, providing comprehensive guidance for living a fulfilling and righteous life.

Q: What role does the Quran play in seeking solutions to health-related issues?

A: The Quran contains verses that emphasize the importance of maintaining good health, seeking medical treatment, and relying on Allah's mercy for healing, offering comfort and guidance during times of illness.

Q: How does listening to the Quran foster a sense of community and unity among believers?

A: Listening to the Quran together in congregational prayers, gatherings, or events fosters a sense of unity, brotherhood, and shared spiritual experience among believers.

Q: Can listening to the Quran enhance concentration and focus?

A: Yes, listening to the Quran with focus and contemplation can improve concentration, sharpen mental clarity, and enhance spiritual awareness, unlike music which may cause distraction and lack of focus.

Q: How does the Quran provide guidance for ethical and moral dilemmas in contemporary society?

A: The Quran contains timeless principles and values that address contemporary ethical and moral challenges, guiding believers towards righteous conduct and virtuous behavior.

Q: What spiritual benefits can be derived from reflecting on the meanings of Quranic verses?

A: Reflecting on the meanings of Quranic verses deepens understanding, strengthens faith, and facilitates personal growth, leading to a closer relationship with Allah and a greater sense of purpose in life.

Q: How does listening to the Quran promote humility and gratitude?

A: Listening to the Quran humbles the heart, reminding us of our dependence on Allah's mercy and blessings, and instills gratitude for His guidance and provisions.

Q: In what ways does the Quran offer solace and hope during times of adversity?

A: The Quran offers solace by reminding believers of Allah's mercy, forgiveness, and promise of reward in the Hereafter, providing hope and resilience in the face of trials and tribulations.

Q: Can the Quran serve as a source of inspiration for personal and spiritual growth?

A: Yes, the Quran inspires believers to strive for excellence in character, deeds, and devotion, guiding them towards continuous self-improvement and spiritual enlightenment.

Q: How does listening to the Quran reinforce Islamic values and principles?

A: Listening to the Quran reinforces Islamic values such as compassion, justice, integrity, and patience, guiding believers to uphold these principles in their daily lives.

Q: What role does the Quran play in fostering a sense of purpose and identity among believers?

A: The Quran provides believers with a sense of purpose by elucidating the meaning of life, the significance of faith, and the importance of fulfilling one's obligations towards Allah and humanity.

Q: Can the Quran serve as a means of seeking forgiveness and repentance?

A: Yes, listening to the Quran prompts believers to reflect on their actions, seek forgiveness for their sins, and renew their commitment to following Allah's guidance, facilitating spiritual growth and purification.

Q: How does the Quran inspire believers to strive for righteousness and excellence in all aspects of life?

A: The Quran encourages believers to emulate the exemplary conduct of the prophets and righteous individuals, motivating them to embody piety, integrity, and compassion in their thoughts, words, and deeds. For more information visit Quranexplains.com or contact Sheikh Touqeer Ansari.

"Choosing Guidance Over Temptation: The Impact of Music on Youth and the Solution in Quranic Listening"

Q: How does listening to music often lead to immoral behavior among youth?

A: Listening to music with explicit lyrics or themes can desensitize youth to moral boundaries, leading to promiscuity, disrespectful behavior, and indulgence in harmful activities.

Q: What are some negative consequences of indulging in music-related activities?

A: Engaging in music-related activities can result in detrimental effects such as substance abuse, involvement in criminal behavior, and strained relationships with family and society.

Q: How does the glorification of materialism in music contribute to negative behaviors among youth?

A: Music often glorifies materialism, leading youth to prioritize wealth, status, and peer approval over moral values, spirituality, and personal growth.

Q: What role does peer pressure play in influencing youth towards music-related behaviors?

A: Peer pressure can compel youth to conform to societal norms and engage in music-related behaviors, even if they contradict their personal beliefs and values.

Q: How does the portrayal of romantic relationships in music impact the behavior of youth?

A: Music often romanticizes unhealthy relationships, unrealistic expectations, and casual intimacy, influencing youth to emulate such behaviors in their own lives.

Q: What are the consequences of youth engaging in drug use or criminal activities associated with music culture?

A: Youth involved in music culture may be more susceptible to drug addiction, criminal behavior, and legal repercussions, resulting in damaged lives and shattered futures.

Q: How does excessive exposure to music contribute to emotional and psychological issues among youth?

A: Excessive exposure to music, especially with negative or explicit content, can exacerbate emotional instability, foster negative attitudes, and contribute to mental health issues like depression and anxiety.

Q: What impact does music-related behavior have on family dynamics and relationships?

A: Music-related behavior can strain family relationships, erode trust, and disrupt household harmony, leading to conflicts, resentment, and breakdowns in communication.

Q: How does the addictive nature of music consumption affect youth and their priorities?

A: The addictive nature of music consumption can distract youth from their responsibilities, hinder personal development, and prioritize instant gratification over long-term goals and aspirations.

Q: What role do parents and educators play in addressing the negative influence of music on youth?

A: Parents and educators have a responsibility to educate youth about the harmful effects of music consumption, set positive examples, and provide alternative outlets for entertainment and self-expression.

Q: How can listening to the Quranic station serve as a solution to music-related issues among youth?

A: Listening to the Quranic station offers a wholesome alternative to music, providing spiritual enrichment, moral guidance, and a sense of peace and tranquility for youth seeking refuge from negative influences.

Q: What benefits can youth derive from replacing music with Quranic listening?

A: Youth can experience spiritual growth, emotional stability, and moral fortitude by immersing themselves in Quranic listening, fostering a deeper connection with their faith and purpose in life.

Q: How does Quranic listening promote positive behavior and character development among youth?

A: Quranic listening instills values of humility, compassion, and self-discipline, encouraging youth to embody virtuous traits and uphold moral principles in their interactions and decisions.

Q: What impact does Quranic listening have on family cohesion and well-being?

A: Quranic listening strengthens family bonds, fosters mutual respect, and promotes harmonious relationships based on shared values and spiritual growth.

Q: How does Quranic listening empower youth to resist negative peer influences and make righteous choices?

A: Quranic listening equips youth with spiritual resilience, moral discernment, and inner strength to resist peer pressure, uphold their beliefs, and navigate life's challenges with integrity and conviction.

Q: How can communities support youth in embracing Quranic listening as a positive lifestyle choice?

A: Communities can create supportive environments that encourage Quranic listening through educational programs, social activities, and access to resources that promote spiritual development and well-being.

Q: What strategies can parents employ to promote Quranic listening as a preferred form of entertainment for their children?

A: Parents can lead by example, establish Quranic listening routines, provide access to quality recitations and translations, and engage in discussions to reinforce the importance of spiritual nourishment.

Q: How does Quranic listening inspire youth to channel their talents and creativity towards positive endeavors?

A: Quranic listening inspires youth to use their talents and creativity in ways that honor their faith, contribute to the betterment of society, and bring fulfillment and satisfaction to their lives.

Q: What spiritual rewards and blessings await youth who prioritize Quranic listening over music?

A: Youth who prioritize Quranic listening over music are rewarded with spiritual enlightenment, divine guidance, and blessings from Allah, paving the way for a fulfilling and purposeful life.

For more information visit Quranexplains.com or contact Sheikh Touqeer Ansari.

"Unveiling the Dangers of Dance: Impact on Society and Spiritual Consequences"

Q: How does the indulgence in dance contribute to the degradation of moral values in society?

A: Indulging in dance often promotes immodesty, encourages inappropriate behavior, and undermines the sanctity of modesty and decency in society.

Q: What role does dance play in perpetuating harmful gender stereotypes and objectification?

A: Dance can reinforce harmful gender stereotypes by portraying women as objects of desire and men as dominant figures, perpetuating inequality and disrespect in relationships.

Q: How does the normalization of dance in mainstream media influence youth perceptions and behaviors?

A: The normalization of dance in mainstream media desensitizes youth to its negative implications, leading them to emulate behaviors that prioritize gratification over moral values and ethics.

Q: What impact does dance culture have on societal norms regarding modesty and chastity?

A: Dance culture often promotes immodesty and promiscuity, eroding societal norms of modesty, chastity, and respect for one's body and others.

Q: How does the glorification of dance in entertainment industries lead to detrimental consequences for youth?

A: The glorification of dance in entertainment industries glamorizes hedonistic lifestyles, trivializes moral values, and encourages reckless behavior among impressionable youth.

Q: What role does peer pressure play in influencing youth to engage in dance-related activities?

A: Peer pressure can compel youth to conform to societal expectations and participate in dance-related activities, even if they contradict their personal beliefs and values.

Q: How does dance contribute to the breakdown of family cohesion and traditional values?

A: Dance activities that promote individualism and self-indulgence can strain family relationships, weaken parental authority, and undermine the transmission of traditional values and cultural heritage.

Q: What impact does the sexualization of dance have on youth perceptions of intimacy and relationships?

A: The sexualization of dance blurs the lines between appropriate and inappropriate forms of intimacy, distorting youth perceptions of healthy relationships and fostering unrealistic expectations.

Q: How does the glorification of dance in educational settings affect academic performance and discipline?

A: The glorification of dance in educational settings can distract students from academic pursuits, disrupt classroom discipline, and hinder overall academic performance.

Q: What psychological effects can arise from the overindulgence in dance-related activities?

A: Overindulgence in dance-related activities can lead to psychological issues such as low self-esteem, body image dissatisfaction, and identity crises among youth.

Q: How does the pursuit of dance as a career path impact societal priorities and values?

A: The pursuit of dance as a career path may prioritize fame, fortune, and personal gratification over contributions to society, moral integrity, and ethical conduct.

Q: What impact does the commercialization of dance have on cultural authenticity and artistic expression?

A: The commercialization of dance can dilute cultural authenticity, perpetuate stereotypes, and exploit artistic expression for profit-driven motives, undermining the integrity of traditional dance forms.

Q: How does the association of dance with substance abuse and other harmful behaviors affect youth well-being?

A: The association of dance culture with substance abuse and other harmful behaviors can jeopardize youth well-being, leading to addiction, legal issues, and long-term health consequences.

Q: What are the spiritual consequences of indulging in dance-related activities contrary to Islamic teachings?

A: Indulging in dance-related activities contrary to Islamic teachings can result in spiritual disconnection, estrangement from Allah's guidance, and a sense of spiritual emptiness and discontent.

Q: How can communities address the negative impact of dance culture on youth and societal values?

A: Communities can promote alternative forms of entertainment and recreation that align with moral values, provide education on the harmful effects of dance culture, and support initiatives that foster cultural enrichment and spiritual growth.

Q: What strategies can parents employ to steer their children away from the harmful influence of dance culture?

A: Parents can foster open communication, set clear boundaries, provide positive role models, and instill Islamic values to guide their children away from the harmful influence of dance culture.

Q: How can educators incorporate discussions about the negative impact of dance culture into school curricula?

A: Educators can integrate discussions about the negative impact of dance culture into school curricula through interdisciplinary approaches, guest speakers, and educational resources that promote critical thinking and moral discernment.

Q: How does promoting alternative forms of entertainment contribute to the well-being of youth and society?

A: Promoting alternative forms of entertainment fosters creativity, intellectual stimulation, and social engagement, contributing to the holistic well-being of youth and reinforcing positive societal values.

Q: What role can religious leaders play in addressing the moral and spiritual consequences of dance culture?

A: Religious leaders can provide guidance, counseling, and spiritual support to individuals struggling with the moral and spiritual consequences of dance culture.

Negative Impact of Dance on Society

Q: How does dance, often accompanied by music, influence people's behavior and actions?

A: Dance, especially when combined with music, can incite powerful emotions and behaviors, sometimes leading to inappropriate or immoral actions.

Q: Why do some parents and elders openly encourage music and dance despite Islamic teachings forbidding them?

A: Some parents and elders may prioritize cultural norms or personal preferences over Islamic teachings, leading them to overlook the negative consequences of music and dance.

Q: What are the societal consequences of embracing music and dance without considering Islamic teachings?

A: Embracing music and dance without adhering to Islamic teachings can lead to moral decay, degradation of values, and societal discord.

Q: How does dance contribute to the objectification and sexualization of individuals, especially among youth?

A: Dance often promotes objectification and sexualization by emphasizing physical appearance and movements that may be suggestive or provocative.

Q: What role does peer pressure play in encouraging youth to participate in dance activities?

A: Peer pressure can compel youth to conform to societal expectations, including participating in dance activities, even if it contradicts Islamic principles.

Q: How does dance culture perpetuate harmful gender stereotypes and expectations?

A: Dance culture may reinforce harmful gender stereotypes by promoting unequal power dynamics, unrealistic beauty standards, and limited roles for individuals based on gender.

Q: What spiritual consequences can arise from engaging in dance activities contrary to Islamic teachings?

A: Engaging in dance activities contrary to Islamic teachings can result in spiritual distancing from Allah, guilt, and a sense of spiritual emptiness or discontent.

Q: How can learning from the Quran and teachings of Prophet Muhammad (peace be upon him) help individuals understand the negative impact of dance?

A: Learning from the Quran and teachings of Prophet Muhammad (peace be upon him) provides guidance on moral conduct, modesty, and the importance of avoiding activities that lead to disobedience to Allah.

Q: What is the significance of Tawheed and Taqwa in guiding individuals away from harmful behaviors like dance?

A: Tawheed (belief in the Oneness of Allah) and Taqwa (God-consciousness) help individuals cultivate a sense of moral responsibility, leading them to avoid behaviors that go against Islamic teachings.

Q: How can children and teenagers understand the importance of adhering to Islamic principles regarding music and dance?

A: Children and teenagers can understand the importance of Islamic principles through age-appropriate education, discussions, and examples set by parents, elders, and religious leaders.

Q: What strategies can parents and elders employ to steer children away from the harmful influence of dance culture?

A: Parents and elders can provide Islamic education, set clear boundaries, monitor media consumption, and foster an environment that promotes adherence to Islamic values.

Q: How can Islamic teachings on modesty and morality serve as a guide for behavior regarding music and dance?

A: Islamic teachings emphasize modesty, decency, and respect for oneself and others, guiding individuals to avoid activities like music and dance that may compromise these values.

Q: What are the long-term consequences of ignoring Islamic teachings regarding music and dance?

A: Ignoring Islamic teachings regarding music and dance can lead to spiritual, moral, and societal consequences, including inner conflict, strained relationships, and distance from Allah.

Q: How can communities and religious leaders address the prevalence of music and dance culture while promoting adherence to Islamic principles?

A: Communities and religious leaders can provide educational programs, offer spiritual guidance, and create supportive environments that encourage adherence to Islamic principles while addressing societal challenges.

Q: What resources are available for individuals seeking to learn more about the Islamic perspective on music and dance?

A: There are numerous Islamic resources, including books, lectures, online courses, and

Islamic scholars, who can provide guidance on understanding and navigating the Islamic perspective on music and dance.

These questions and answers provide insights into the negative impact of dance on society and offer solutions rooted in Islamic teachings for individuals, parents, and communities to address this issue effectively. For more information visit Quranexplains.com or contact Sheikh Touqeer Ansari.

Song Music, Dance Lovers, Learn; WHY ISLAM?

What makes songs, music, and dance tempting to individuals?

Songs, music, and dance often appeal to people's senses and emotions, offering temporary pleasure and escape from reality.

How do songs, music, and dance contribute to societal disasters?

They can lead individuals astray from moral values, encouraging behavior that is harmful to themselves and society.

What role does peer pressure play in the consumption of songs, music, and dance?

Peer pressure can compel individuals to engage in these activities to fit in with their social circles, even if they recognize the potential harm.

How do songs, music, and dance affect mental health?

They can contribute to addiction, depression, and anxiety, especially when used as coping mechanisms for deeper emotional issues.

What are the consequences of excessive exposure to explicit lyrics and inappropriate content in songs and music?

It can desensitize individuals to violence, objectification, and other negative behaviors portrayed in the media.

How does the glamorization of materialism and superficiality in songs and music impact societal values?

It can promote a culture of consumerism, leading to shallow priorities and a lack of focus on meaningful aspects of life.

What dangers do sexually suggestive lyrics and provocative dance moves pose to young audiences?

They can normalize unhealthy attitudes towards relationships, sexuality, and consent, leading to early sexualization and risky behavior.

How do songs, music, and dance contribute to the erosion of traditional cultural values?

They can overshadow traditional cultural expressions and promote Westernized ideals that may not align with local customs and beliefs.

What role does parental guidance play in mitigating the negative effects of songs, music, and dance?

Parents can educate their children about discerning between appropriate and inappropriate content and provide alternative forms of entertainment.

Are there any positive aspects to songs, music, and dance that counterbalance their negative impact?

While some argue for their artistic and entertainment value, the potential harm they pose often outweighs any perceived benefits.

How can educational institutions address the influence of songs, music, and dance on students?

Schools can incorporate media literacy and critical thinking skills into their curriculum to help students analyze and question the messages portrayed in songs, music, and dance.

What strategies can individuals use to resist the temptation of songs, music, and dance?

They can cultivate self-awareness, develop alternative hobbies, seek support from like-minded peers, and set boundaries regarding their media consumption.

Do religious teachings offer any guidance on the consumption of songs, music, and dance?

Many religious traditions caution against indulging in activities that lead to moral corruption and distance from spiritual values.

How do songs, music, and dance impact interpersonal relationships and social dynamics?

They can influence how individuals interact with one another, shaping attitudes, behaviors, and perceptions of social norms.

What role does media regulation play in addressing the harmful impact of songs, music, and dance?

Governments and regulatory bodies can implement policies to restrict access to explicit content and promote media literacy among the populace.

Can exposure to songs, music, and dance lead to desensitization to violence and other negative behaviors?

Yes, repeated exposure can normalize harmful behaviors, making individuals less sensitive to their consequences.

How do songs, music, and dance affect the development of children and adolescents?

They can shape their worldview, influence their attitudes towards gender roles, relationships, and societal norms, and impact their emotional well-being.

What responsibility do artists and media producers have in mitigating the harmful impact of songs, music, and dance?

They should consider the ethical implications of their content and strive to create art that uplifts, inspires, and promotes positive values.

How can communities work together to address the root causes of the harmful impact of songs, music, and dance?

By fostering open dialogue, promoting media literacy, and providing support systems for individuals struggling with addiction or negative influences.

In what ways can individuals advocate for change and raise awareness about the harmful impact of songs, music, and dance?

They can participate in activism, support organizations that promote positive media representation, and engage in discussions within their communities about responsible media consumption. Except slam, all the Religions based on songs, music and dance except Islamic Values leads towards spiritual guidance more info visit; QuranExplains.com or contact Sh Touqeer ANSARi

"Tune of Temptation: The Harmful Impact of Songs, Music, or Dance" Excluding Islamic Values Leading to Family Disasters

How do explicit lyrics and suggestive content in songs and music contribute to family conflicts?

Exposure to such content can lead to disagreements between family members, especially between parents and children, regarding acceptable media consumption.

What role does excessive use of social media and online platforms for sharing dance videos play in family dynamics?

It can lead to reduced family interaction and communication as individuals spend more time engrossed in virtual entertainment rather than engaging with their families.

How do unrealistic portrayals of relationships and lifestyles in songs, music, and dance impact family expectations and satisfaction?

They can create unrealistic expectations within families, leading to dissatisfaction with one's own life and relationships when they don't match up to the glamorous depictions in media.

What dangers do addictive behaviors towards songs, music, or dance pose to family cohesion and stability?

Addiction to entertainment can lead to neglect of familial responsibilities, strained relationships, and financial troubles due to excessive spending on concerts, events, or merchandise.

How does the normalization of substance abuse and party culture in songs, music, or dance influence family values and priorities?

It can lead to conflicts within families as individuals may prioritize socializing and partying over familial obligations, risking their well-being and stability.

What impact does the objectification of individuals, especially women, in songs, music, or dance have on family dynamics and respect?

It can lead to the perpetuation of harmful gender stereotypes and disrespect towards family members, particularly women, as they may be viewed as mere objects of desire rather than equal partners in the family unit.

How does the portrayal of violence and aggression in songs, music, or dance affect family relationships and communication?

Exposure to violent content can desensitize individuals, leading to increased aggression and conflict resolution issues within the family.

What role does peer pressure to engage in certain types of music, dance, or social activities play in straining family relationships?

It can create tension within families as individuals may feel pressured to conform to their peers' expectations, even if it goes against their family's values and beliefs.

How does the commercialization of music and dance industries contribute to family financial strains and disputes?

Excessive spending on concerts, merchandise, or dance classes can lead to financial difficulties within families, resulting in arguments over budgeting and financial priorities.

What steps can families take to mitigate the negative impact of songs, music, or dance on their relationships and well-being?

Families can establish open communication channels, set boundaries regarding media consumption, engage in shared activities that promote bonding, and seek professional help if needed to address addiction or conflict issues.

For more information visit Quranexplains.com or contact Sheikh Touqeer Ansari.

Dangers of Satanic Music and Dance

What are the potential dangers of listening to Satanic songs or engaging in hip hop music and dance? What Muslims faced in western society

Exposure to explicit lyrics and negative messages that glorify violence, substance abuse, and immoral behavior.

How can Satanic songs or hip hop music influence teenagers' behavior?

They can desensitize teenagers to violence, promote disrespectful attitudes towards authority, and encourage rebellious behavior.

What role does peer pressure play in teenagers' engagement with Satanic songs and hip hop culture?

Peer pressure can compel teenagers to conform to societal norms associated with these genres, leading them down a destructive path.

How do Satanic songs and hip hop culture impact teenagers' mental health?

They can contribute to depression, anxiety, and feelings of isolation by promoting negative self-image and unrealistic standards.

What are the consequences of teenagers getting involved in Satanic rituals or cults through music and dance?

They risk alienating themselves from their families, facing legal repercussions, and falling into a cycle of destructive behavior.

How can parents recognize if their teenagers are being influenced by Satanic songs or hip hop culture?

Signs may include changes in behavior, attitude, or appearance, as well as a sudden disinterest in school or family activities.

What steps can teenagers take to resist the allure of Satanic songs and hip hop culture?

They can seek positive influences, engage in alternative activities, and surround themselves with supportive peers and mentors.

How can schools and communities address the issue of Satanic songs and hip hop influence among teenagers?

By providing education on critical thinking, media literacy, and positive role modeling to counteract negative influences.

What are some positive alternatives to Satanic songs and hip hop music for teenagers?

Engaging in creative outlets like art, sports, or volunteering, and exploring genres with uplifting messages and themes.

How can teenagers protect themselves from the psychological manipulation often present in Satanic songs and hip hop culture?

By developing strong self-esteem, critical thinking skills, and a sense of identity grounded in positive values.

Are there any long-term consequences for teenagers who become involved in Satanic songs or hip hop culture?

Yes, they may face challenges in building healthy relationships, pursuing education and career goals, and overall personal development.

What support systems are available for teenagers who want to break free from the influence of Satanic songs and hip hop culture?

Counseling services, support groups, and community organizations can provide guidance and assistance in navigating these challenges.

How can teenagers educate their peers about the dangers of Satanic songs and hip hop culture without being judgmental?

By initiating open and honest conversations, sharing personal experiences, and providing resources for further exploration.

What impact can parental involvement have on teenagers' susceptibility to Satanic songs and hip hop culture?

Positive parental involvement, including setting clear boundaries, fostering open communication, and being role models, can mitigate the influence of negative external factors.

Are there any success stories of teenagers who have overcome the influence of Satanic songs and hip hop culture?

Yes, many teenagers have successfully redirected their focus towards positive activities and values, leading to personal growth and fulfillment.

How does the portrayal of women in Satanic songs and hip hop culture affect teenagers' perceptions of gender roles and relationships?

It can perpetuate harmful stereotypes, objectification, and disrespect towards women, influencing teenagers' attitudes and behaviors.

What role does media consumption play in teenagers' exposure to Satanic songs and hip hop culture?

Excessive media consumption, particularly of violent or explicit content, can desensitize teenagers and normalize destructive behaviors.

What strategies can teenagers use to resist the pressure to conform to Satanic songs and hip hop culture while still maintaining social connections?

By seeking out like-minded peers, setting personal boundaries, and expressing their individuality through positive outlets.

How can teenagers differentiate between artistic expression and harmful messages in Satanic songs and hip hop culture?

By critically analyzing lyrics, considering the context and intent behind the music, and recognizing the potential impact on themselves and others.

What role does self-reflection play in teenagers' ability to recognize and resist the influence of Satanic songs and hip hop culture?

Self-reflection allows teenagers to evaluate their beliefs, values, and behaviors, empowering them to make informed choices aligned with their personal growth and well-being.

For more information visit Quranexplains.com or contact Sheikh Touqeer Ansari.

Music, Dance & Songs Contributes to Loss of Faith

How do songs, music, and dance contribute to the loss of faith among Muslim teenagers?

Exposure to lyrics, themes, and behaviors contradictory to Islamic values can weaken teenagers' faith over time.

What role do songs, music, and dance play in influencing teenagers' attitudes towards religion and spirituality?

They can desensitize teenagers to the importance of religious principles and foster a secular worldview.

How can parents be held responsible for their teenagers' loss of faith due to exposure to songs, music, and dance?

Parents who fail to monitor their children's media consumption or provide proper guidance may inadvertently contribute to their loss of faith.

What are some common themes in songs, music, and dance that contradict Islamic beliefs?

Themes of materialism, promiscuity, substance abuse, and rebellion against authority are often glorified in mainstream media.

How can songs, music, and dance contribute to the erosion of teenagers' mental health, sans mental illness?

Exposure to negative themes and behaviors can lead to feelings of alienation, depression, and anxiety, even in mentally healthy individuals.

What steps can parents take to protect their teenagers from the negative influence of songs, music, and dance?

Setting clear boundaries, monitoring media consumption, and fostering open communication about Islamic values and beliefs.

How does a lack of understanding of Tawheed and Taqwa contribute to teenagers' vulnerability to songs, music, and dance?

Without a solid foundation in Islamic principles, teenagers may be more susceptible to the allure of worldly pleasures promoted in mainstream media.

What are some warning signs that a Muslim teenager may be losing their faith

due to exposure to songs, music, and dance?

Signs may include a decline in religious observance, increased interest in secular activities, and questioning of Islamic teachings.

Can exposure to songs, music, and dance lead to religious confusion among Muslim teenagers?

Yes, conflicting messages between Islamic teachings and secular media can create confusion about religious identity and beliefs.

How can Islamic education and community involvement help protect Muslim teenagers from the negative influence of songs, music, and dance?

By providing a strong foundation in Islamic teachings, fostering a sense of belonging, and offering positive alternatives to mainstream media.

What role does peer pressure play in influencing Muslim teenagers' engagement with songs, music, and dance?

Peer pressure can compel teenagers to conform to societal norms, even if they contradict Islamic values.

Are there any positive aspects of songs, music, and dance that Muslim teenagers

can engage in without compromising their faith?

Yes, there are Islamic alternatives to mainstream media that promote positive messages and align with Islamic values.

How can Muslim teenagers balance their desire for cultural engagement with the need to uphold Islamic principles?

By seeking out halal forms of entertainment, maintaining a strong connection to their faith, and surrounding themselves with supportive peers.

What impact can parental involvement have on Muslim teenagers' understanding of Tawheed and Taqwa?

Positive parental involvement, including modeling Islamic values and providing religious education, can reinforce teenagers' faith and resilience.

Are there any Islamic teachings or stories that can help Muslim teenagers navigate the challenges posed by songs, music, and dance?

Yes, stories of the prophets and their struggles against temptation, as well as teachings on the importance of guarding one's faith, can provide guidance.

How can Muslim teenagers develop a stronger sense of Tawheed and Taqwa in the face of societal pressures?

By engaging in regular worship, seeking knowledge, and surrounding themselves with positive influences.

What role does self-awareness play in helping Muslim teenagers recognize the negative impact of songs, music, and dance on their faith?

Self-awareness allows teenagers to reflect on their choices and behaviors, empowering them to make informed decisions aligned with their faith.

How can Muslim teenagers seek forgiveness and redemption if they have strayed from their faith due to exposure to songs, music, and dance?

By sincerely repenting, seeking guidance from knowledgeable individuals, and striving to realign their actions with Islamic teachings.

What support systems are available for Muslim teenagers struggling with the influence of songs, music, and dance on their faith?

Counseling services, youth groups, and Islamic organizations can provide guidance, support, and a sense of community.

How can Muslim teenagers use their experiences with songs, music, and dance as opportunities for spiritual growth and development?

By reflecting on their experiences, learning from their mistakes, and striving to deepen their understanding and practice of Islamic principles.

For more information visit Quranexplains.com or contact Sheikh Touqeer Ansari.

Examples of Satanic Themes of Music & Dance

What are some examples of Satanic themes or messages that may be present in songs, music, or dance?

Satanic themes may include glorification of immorality, violence, rebellion against authority, or explicit references to occult practices.

How can exposure to Satanic songs, music, or dance impact teenagers' beliefs and behaviors?

Exposure to such content can desensitize teenagers to moral values, promote negative attitudes and behaviors, and lead them away from the teachings of Islam.

Why is it important for teenagers to be aware of the potential dangers associated with Satanic songs, music, or dance?

Awareness helps teenagers make informed choices about the media they consume and safeguards their spiritual and moral well-being.

What role does Tawheed play in protecting teenagers from the influence of Satanic content?

Tawheed reinforces the belief in the Oneness of Allah and strengthens teenagers' resilience against Satanic temptations by prioritizing their devotion to Him.

How can teenagers cultivate Taqwa to shield themselves from the allure of Satanic songs, music, or dance?

Taqwa fosters God-consciousness, guiding teenagers to avoid harmful influences and adhere to righteous behavior in all aspects of life.

What are some practical steps teenagers can take to avoid exposure to Satanic songs, music, or dance?

Teens can be mindful of the media they consume, seek alternatives with positive messages, and engage in activities aligned with Islamic values.

How can QuranExplains.com serve as a resource for teenagers seeking to learn about Tawheed and Taqwa?

QuranExplains.com offers comprehensive explanations of Quranic teachings, providing teenagers with valuable insights into Tawheed and Taqwa.

What are some warning signs that a song, music, or dance may contain Satanic influences?

Warning signs may include explicit lyrics, dark imagery, occult symbols, or messages that contradict Islamic principles.

How can teenagers critically analyze the content of songs, music, or dance to determine if they align with Islamic values?

Teens can assess lyrics, themes, and symbolism, considering whether they promote virtues or encourage sinful behavior.

What impact can exposure to Satanic songs, music, or dance have on teenagers' mental and emotional well-being?

Exposure can contribute to feelings of anxiety, depression, or spiritual emptiness, undermining teenagers' overall mental health.

How can parents and educators support teenagers in navigating the influence of Satanic content in today's media landscape?

Adults can provide guidance, set boundaries, and offer alternative forms of entertainment that promote positive values and beliefs.

Why is it important for teenagers to seek knowledge about Islam and strengthen their faith in the face of societal pressures?

Knowledge empowers teenagers to make informed decisions and resist negative influences, fostering spiritual growth and resilience.

What role does peer influence play in teenagers' susceptibility to Satanic songs, music, or dance?

Peer pressure can exacerbate teenagers' vulnerability to negative influences, making it crucial for them to choose friends who uphold Islamic values.

How can teenagers use their creativity and talents to promote positive messages through songs, music, or dance?

Teens can create or support content that celebrates Islamic values, fosters unity, and inspires others to lead righteous lives.

What are some consequences of indulging in Satanic songs, music, or dance, both in this life and the Hereafter?

Consequences may include moral degradation, loss of spiritual fulfillment, and accountability before Allah on the Day of Judgment.

How can teenagers strike a balance between enjoying cultural expressions and safeguarding their faith from harmful influences?

Teens can appreciate cultural diversity while being discerning about the content they consume, ensuring it aligns with Islamic principles.

What are some strategies teenagers can use to resist peer pressure to engage in activities contrary to their religious beliefs?

Teens can assert their values respectfully, seek support from like-minded peers, and focus on activities that reinforce their faith.

How can teenagers engage in constructive dialogue with friends or peers who may not share their religious convictions about the influence of music and dance?

Teens can share their perspectives respectfully, provide factual information, and emphasize the importance of personal convictions in decision-making.

What resources or support networks are available for teenagers who may struggle with addiction or dependency on Satanic songs, music, or dance?

Teens can seek guidance from trusted adults, access counseling services, and connect with religious communities for support and guidance.

In what ways can teenagers use social media platforms and online communities to promote awareness about the dangers of Satanic content and foster positive change?

Teens can share informative posts, participate in online discussions, and collaborate with peers to raise awareness and advocate for healthier media consumption habits.

For more information visit Quranexplains.com or contact Sheikh Touqeer Ansari.

"Dancing with the Devil: Exposing the Immorality of Music and Dance"

What are some examples of sexual violence themes present in songs, music, or dance?

Songs, music, or dance may contain lyrics, imagery, or choreography that glorifies or trivializes sexual violence, coercion, or abuse.

How can exposure to songs, music, or dance featuring sexual violence themes impact children's understanding of morality and ethics?

Exposure can desensitize children to the seriousness of sexual violence, distort their perceptions of healthy relationships, and erode their moral compass.

Why is it crucial for Muslim parents to protect their children from the influence of songs, music, or dance promoting sexual violence?

It is crucial because such content contradicts Islamic teachings on modesty, respect, and consent, and can lead children astray from their faith.

What role does Tawheed play in safeguarding children's faith against the immorality of sexual violence content?

Tawheed reinforces the belief in the Oneness of Allah, emphasizing the importance of upholding His commands, including principles of modesty and respect for others.

How can parents use QuranExplains.com to educate their children about Tawheed and Taqwa as protection against immoral content?

Parents can utilize QuranExplains.com to access detailed explanations of Quranic teachings on Tawheed and Taqwa, providing children with a strong foundation to discern right from wrong.

What are some warning signs that a song, music, or dance may contain themes of sexual violence?

Warning signs may include explicit lyrics, suggestive imagery, objectification of individuals, or normalization of abusive behavior.

How can parents initiate conversations with their children about the dangers of songs, music, or dance featuring sexual violence themes?

Parents can initiate age-appropriate discussions, emphasize Islamic values, and encourage critical thinking to help children understand the harmful effects of such content.

What proactive steps can parents take to limit their children's exposure to songs, music, or dance promoting sexual violence?

Parents can monitor children's media consumption, use parental controls, provide alternative forms of entertainment, and foster open communication about media choices.

How can children differentiate between appropriate and inappropriate content in songs, music, or dance?

Children can learn to analyze lyrics, imagery, and messages critically, considering whether they align with Islamic values of modesty, respect, and compassion.

What impact can exposure to sexual violence themes in songs, music, or dance have on children's mental and emotional well-being?

Exposure can lead to feelings of confusion, anxiety, and desensitization to violence, potentially affecting children's emotional development and psychological health.

How can Taqwa guide children in making ethical choices and resisting the allure of immoral content?

Taqwa fosters God-consciousness, guiding children to uphold moral principles, respect others' dignity, and avoid behaviors that contradict Islamic teachings.

What resources or support networks are available for parents seeking guidance on protecting their children from harmful media content?

Parents can seek support from Islamic organizations, parenting forums, and educational resources that provide guidance on media literacy and child protection.

How can parents foster a home environment that promotes Islamic values and shields children from the influence of immoral media content?

Parents can model virtuous behavior, create family rituals centered on Islamic teachings, and establish clear boundaries regarding media consumption.

What role can Islamic schools or community centers play in educating children about the dangers of immoral media content?

Islamic schools or community centers can provide educational programs, workshops, and resources that address media literacy, critical thinking, and moral development.

How can children use their creativity and talents to produce or support media content that promotes positive values and behaviors?

Children can create artwork, music, or other forms of media that convey messages of kindness, empathy, and respect, contributing to a culture of positivity and virtue.

Why is it essential for children to seek guidance from trusted adults when encountering media content that makes them uncomfortable or raises questions?

Seeking guidance ensures children receive accurate information, emotional support, and practical strategies for navigating challenging media content in a safe and responsible manner.

How can parents and educators collaborate to develop media literacy skills in children and empower them to make informed choices about media consumption?

Parents and educators can collaborate on workshops, discussions, and educational initiatives that teach children how to critically evaluate media content and make responsible choices.

What are some Islamic teachings or principles that children can apply when evaluating the appropriateness of songs, music, or dance?

Children can apply teachings on modesty, respect for others, honesty, and compassion when evaluating media content and its alignment with Islamic values.

How can children use social media platforms and online communities to advocate for ethical media consumption and raise awareness about the dangers of immoral content?

Children can share positive messages, engage in discussions, and collaborate with peers to promote ethical media consumption and counteract harmful influences online.

What are the long-term consequences of exposing children to songs, music, or dance featuring themes of sexual violence, both in this life and the Hereafter?

Consequences may include desensitization to violence, erosion of moral character, and accountability before Allah for the choices made regarding media consumption.

Examples of Satanic Whispers in Dance

What are some examples of Satanic whispers present in songs, music, or dance?

Satanic whispers in songs, music, or dance may include lyrics promoting immoral behavior, glorifying materialism, or encouraging disobedience to Allah.

How can the recitation of Quran protect Muslims, especially children and teenagers, from Satanic influences in songs, music, or dance?

The recitation of Quran acts as a shield against Satanic whispers, purifying the heart and mind, and strengthening one's connection with Allah.

What specific verses or chapters of the Quran are recommended for protection against Satanic whispers?

Surah Al-Falaq (Chapter 113) and Surah An-Nas (Chapter 114) are specifically recommended for seeking refuge from Satanic whispers and evil influences.

How does the recitation of Quran instill Tawheed (Oneness of Allah) and Taqwa

(God-consciousness) in individuals, particularly children and teenagers?

The recitation of Quran reinforces the belief in the Oneness of Allah and fosters God-consciousness by reminding individuals of Allah's greatness, mercy, and guidance.

Can children and teenagers benefit from listening to the Quran regularly, even if they may not understand its meaning fully?

Yes, children and teenagers can benefit from listening to the Quran regularly as the sound of Quranic recitation has a profound effect on the heart and soul, even if they may not comprehend its meaning fully.

How can parents incorporate the recitation of Quran into their children's daily routine to protect them from Satanic influences?

Parents can encourage their children to listen to Quranic recitation during their daily activities, such as in the morning, before bedtime, or while commuting.

What role can memorizing and understanding the meaning of Quranic verses play in safeguarding children and teenagers from Satanic whispers?

Memorizing and understanding the meaning of Quranic verses empowers children and teenagers to recognize Satanic whispers and resist them with knowledge and faith.

How can parents and educators create a conducive environment for children and teenagers to engage with the Quran regularly?

Parents and educators can set aside dedicated time for Quranic recitation, provide resources for learning and memorization, and serve as positive role models in their own Quranic practices.

What are some practical tips for children and teenagers to develop a habit of reciting Quran regularly for protection from Satanic influences?

Children and teenagers can start by reciting small portions of the Quran daily, seeking help from parents or teachers for pronunciation and meaning, and gradually increasing their recitation as they progress.

How can the recitation of Quran serve as a source of comfort and solace for children and teenagers facing challenges or difficulties?

The melodious recitation of Quranic verses can bring peace and tranquility to the hearts of children and teenagers, offering them strength and guidance in times of need.

In what ways can parents and educators integrate the teachings of Quran into children's lives to reinforce protection from Satanic whispers in songs, music, or dance?

Parents and educators can use Quranic stories, lessons, and moral teachings to instill values of righteousness, integrity, and resilience in children, helping them discern between right and wrong.

How does the recitation of Quran promote spiritual growth and development in children and teenagers?

The recitation of Quran nurtures a deep connection with Allah, fosters humility and gratitude, and cultivates a sense of purpose and direction in life for children and teenagers.

What are some common misconceptions about the recitation of Quran for protection against Satanic influences?

Some misconceptions may include believing that listening to Quranic recitation is only beneficial for adults or that understanding the meaning of Quranic verses is necessary for its efficacy.

How can parents and educators encourage children and teenagers to seek refuge in the Quran when faced with temptations or peer pressure related to songs, music, or dance?

Parents and educators can remind children and teenagers of the protective power of Quranic recitation, encourage them to recite specific verses for guidance and strength, and provide emotional support and guidance during challenging situations.

What are the spiritual benefits of reciting Quran together as a family or community for protection against Satanic influences?

Reciting Quran together fosters unity, strengthens family bonds, and invokes Allah's blessings and protection upon the entire family or community.

How can children and teenagers develop a deeper connection with the Quran beyond mere recitation for protection from Satanic whispers?

Children and teenagers can engage in activities such as memorization, reflection on Quranic verses, seeking knowledge about its interpretation, and implementing its teachings in their daily lives.

What are some examples of stories from the Quran that highlight the consequences

of succumbing to Satanic whispers and the importance of seeking protection through Quranic recitation?

Examples may include the story of Prophet Yusuf (Joseph) and his resistance to temptation, or the story of Prophet Muhammad (peace be upon him) seeking refuge from Satan's influence during his prophetic mission.

How can parents and educators address children's questions or concerns about Satanic influences in songs, music, or dance through Quranic teachings?

Parents and educators can provide age-appropriate explanations, share relevant Quranic verses and stories, and encourage open dialogue to help children understand and navigate such influences in accordance with Islamic principles.

What are some practical strategies for incorporating Quranic recitation into children's educational settings, such as Islamic schools or homeschooling environments?

Strategies may include integrating Quranic recitation into daily routines, organizing Quranic recitation competitions or events, and providing resources for Quranic learning and memorization.

In what ways can children and teenagers share the benefits of Quranic recitation with their peers or classmates to promote protection against Satanic influences collectively?

Children and teenagers can organize Quran study groups, lead Quranic recitation sessions, and encourage their peers to explore the spiritual and protective benefits of engaging with the Quran together.

For more information visit Quranexplains.com or contact Sheikh Touqeer Ansari.

"Rotten Rhythms: Exploring the Sinister Nature of Satanic Whispers in Song, Music, and Dance"

How can Satan influence Muslims to deviate from Tawheed through secularism and education?

Satan can exploit secular ideologies and education systems to promote disbelief in Allah and divert Muslims from their faith.

What are some worldly temptations that Satan uses to distract Muslims from focusing on Taqwa?

Satan entices Muslims with materialistic pursuits, such as wealth, fame, and indulgence in worldly pleasures, leading them away from the path of righteousness.

How does Satan use parties and social gatherings as a means to corrupt Muslim beliefs and behavior?

Satan promotes immoral behavior at parties, encouraging Muslims to engage in activities contrary to Islamic teachings, such as mixing with the opposite sex without marriage and excessive consumption of intoxicants.

What role do songs, music, and dance play in amplifying Satan's influence on Muslims?

Songs, music, and dance serve as mediums through which Satan spreads his whispers, captivating individuals and leading them towards sinful behavior and spiritual degradation.

How can teenagers and adults distinguish between lawful and unlawful forms of entertainment in the context of Islamic teachings?

By referring to Quranic principles and prophetic guidance, Muslims can discern whether certain forms of entertainment align with Islamic values or promote disobedience to Allah.

What are the consequences of succumbing to the allure of songs, music, and dance as influenced by Satan?

Muslims risk drifting away from the remembrance of Allah, weakening their faith, and falling into sinful behavior that distances them from the path of Taqwa.

In what ways can Muslims protect themselves from Satanic whispers conveyed through songs, music, and dance?

Muslims can safeguard themselves by seeking refuge in Allah, increasing their knowledge of Islamic teachings, and avoiding environments conducive to sinful behavior.

How can parents and educators guide teenagers and adults in understanding the harmful effects of Satanic whispers in songs, music, and dance?

Parents and educators can educate individuals about the deceptive nature of worldly pleasures and emphasize the importance of adhering to Islamic values in all aspects of life.

What strategies can Muslims employ to counteract the influence of Satanic whispers and strengthen their commitment to Tawheed and Taqwa?

Muslims can engage in regular Quranic recitation, establish a strong connection with Allah through prayer and supplication, and seek knowledge from reputable Islamic sources.

How does the concept of accountability in the Hereafter serve as a deterrent against succumbing to Satanic whispers in songs, music, and dance?

Belief in the Day of Judgment reminds Muslims of their ultimate accountability before Allah, motivating them to resist temptations and prioritize actions that please Him.

What advice can be given to teenagers and adults who struggle with the influence of Satanic whispers in their entertainment choices?

They should seek support from knowledgeable mentors or counselors, engage in self-reflection and repentance, and strive to replace sinful habits with virtuous actions that draw them closer to Allah.

How can community leaders and Islamic scholars play a role in raising awareness about the dangers of Satanic whispers in songs, music, and dance?

They can deliver sermons, conduct educational workshops, and utilize social media platforms to disseminate information and provide guidance on resisting Satan's influence.

What role does self-discipline play in protecting oneself from Satanic whispers in entertainment?

Self-discipline helps individuals resist impulsive urges and make conscious decisions aligned with Islamic principles, thereby guarding against the allure of Satanic whispers.

How can Muslims strike a balance between enjoying permissible forms of entertainment and safeguarding themselves from Satanic influences?

By exercising moderation, being mindful of the content and environment of entertainment activities, and constantly seeking Allah's guidance and protection.

What are some Quranic verses and prophetic sayings that highlight the importance of guarding against Satanic whispers in all aspects of life, including entertainment?

Verses such as Surah Al-Baqarah (2:168) and Hadiths emphasizing the dangers of following one's desires without regard for Islamic principles serve as reminders for Muslims to remain vigilant against Satan's influence.

How can the Islamic concept of seeking forgiveness (Tawbah) help individuals who have been affected by Satanic whispers in songs, music, and dance?

Seeking forgiveness allows individuals to acknowledge their mistakes, repent sincerely, and strive to rectify their behavior, thereby seeking Allah's mercy and protection from further harm.

What are some practical steps that individuals can take to reduce their exposure to Satanic whispers in entertainment in today's digital age?

They can filter their media consumption, surround themselves with virtuous company, and prioritize activities that promote spiritual growth and well-being.

Why is it crucial for Muslims to be vigilant and proactive in combating Satanic whispers, especially in the realm of entertainment?

Failing to recognize and resist Satanic whispers can lead to spiritual decline, moral corruption, and ultimately, estrangement from Allah and His guidance.

How does fostering a strong sense of Islamic identity and community cohesion help individuals resist the influence of Satanic whispers in songs, music, and dance?

A strong Islamic identity provides a moral compass and support network, enabling individuals to withstand societal pressures and remain steadfast in their faith and values.

In what ways can individuals support each other in their efforts to overcome the influence of Satanic whispers and cultivate a strong connection with Allah?

By fostering a supportive environment, encouraging each other in faith-based activities, and reminding one another of the importance of seeking Allah's guidance and protection.

Satan's Symphony: The Subversion of Tawheed and Taqwa Through Songs, Music, and Dance

How does Satan utilize secularism and education to erode Muslims' understanding of Tawheed?

Satan exploits secular ideologies and educational systems to divert Muslims' focus away from Allah, leading them towards atheism or agnosticism.

What worldly desires and temptations does Satan use to distract Muslims from Tawheed?

Satan tempts Muslims with the pursuit of wealth, fame, and materialistic gains, shifting their priorities away from worshipping Allah and towards fulfilling worldly desires.

How does the absence of belief in the Hereafter contribute to the destruction of Tawheed among Muslims?

Without belief in the Hereafter, Muslims may become consumed by worldly pursuits and neglect their spiritual obligations, thereby weakening their adherence to Tawheed.

In what ways does Satan manipulate entertainment, such as parties, to undermine Muslims' understanding of Taqwa?

Satan promotes immoral behavior at parties, enticing Muslims to engage in forbidden activities like fornication and mingling with the opposite sex, leading them away from the path of Taqwa.

How do songs, music, and dance serve as tools for Satan to corrupt the minds and hearts of Muslims?

Satan utilizes the captivating power of music and dance to instill sinful thoughts and desires in Muslims, leading them astray from the teachings of Islam and towards disobedience to Allah.

What role do parents and educators play in protecting teenagers from the influence of Satanic whispers in entertainment?

Parents and educators must educate teenagers about the harmful effects of sinful entertainment, instill Islamic values, and provide guidance on making righteous choices.

How can teenagers discern between permissible and impermissible forms of entertainment in light of Islamic teachings?

By referring to the Quran and Sunnah, teenagers can evaluate entertainment options based on whether they align with Islamic principles of modesty, morality, and obedience to Allah.

What are the consequences of indulging in sinful entertainment for teenagers' spiritual well-being?

Indulging in sinful entertainment can lead teenagers away from the path of righteousness, causing spiritual decay, moral corruption, and distance from Allah.

How can teenagers strengthen their Tawheed and Taqwa amidst the pervasive influence of Satanic whispers in society?

Teenagers can strengthen their faith by engaging in regular worship, seeking knowledge about Islam, surrounding themselves with righteous company, and seeking Allah's protection through prayer.

What practical steps can teenagers take to resist the allure of sinful entertainment and uphold their commitment to Tawheed and Taqwa?

Teenagers can avoid environments where sinful entertainment is prevalent, engage in wholesome activities, and cultivate a strong connection with Allah through remembrance and supplication.

Why is it essential for teenagers to prioritize their spiritual well-being over worldly pleasures and desires?

Prioritizing spiritual well-being ensures teenagers' long-term happiness, fulfillment, and success in both this life and the Hereafter, unlike fleeting worldly pleasures.

How does the concept of accountability in the Hereafter serve as a deterrent against succumbing to Satanic whispers in entertainment?

Belief in the Day of Judgment reminds teenagers of their ultimate accountability before Allah, motivating them to resist temptations and prioritize actions that please Him.

What are the benefits of seeking refuge in Allah from Satanic whispers in entertainment?

Seeking refuge in Allah protects teenagers from the influence of Satanic whispers, strengthens their resolve to uphold Islamic values, and draws them closer to Allah's mercy and guidance.

How can teenagers overcome peer pressure to engage in sinful entertainment and instead foster environments of righteousness?

Teenagers can seek support from like-minded friends, set boundaries with peers who promote sinful behavior, and lead by example in promoting virtuous activities.

What role do Islamic scholars and community leaders play in raising awareness about the dangers of Satanic whispers in entertainment?

Islamic scholars and community leaders must educate teenagers about the harms of sinful entertainment, provide guidance on navigating societal influences, and offer support in strengthening faith.

How can teenagers utilize technology and social media platforms to spread awareness about the importance of guarding against Satanic whispers?

Teenagers can use technology and social media to share Islamic teachings, promote virtuous content, and engage in discussions about the detrimental effects of sinful entertainment.

Why is ongoing self-reflection and repentance crucial for teenagers who may have been influenced by Satanic whispers in entertainment?

Self-reflection and repentance enable teenagers to acknowledge their mistakes, seek forgiveness from Allah, and commit to positive change, thereby renewing their commitment to Tawheed and Taqwa.

What role do parents play in monitoring and guiding their teenagers' entertainment choices to ensure they align with Islamic values?

Parents must supervise their teenagers' media consumption, provide guidance on discerning between right and wrong, and foster open communication to address any concerns or questions.

How can teenagers cultivate a love for Quranic recitation and Islamic knowledge to strengthen their immunity against Satanic whispers?

Teenagers can participate in Quranic study circles, listen to Islamic lectures and podcasts, and incorporate regular Quranic recitation and memorization into their daily routines.

What advice would you give to teenagers who strive to maintain their faith and integrity in the face of societal pressures and temptations?

Stay steadfast in faith, seek guidance from Allah through prayer and supplication, surround yourself with righteous influences, and remember that Allah's pleasure is the ultimate goal worth striving for. Learn more about Tawheed and Taqwa get way to Paradise visit QuranExplains.com or contact Sh;Touqeer ANSARi.

"Preserving Taqwa: The Role of Muslims in Resisting the Temptations of Songs, Music, and Dance"

What is the significance of Taqwa in the life of a Muslim, and why is it important to preserve it?

Taqwa represents consciousness of Allah and is essential for a Muslim's spiritual well-being and adherence to Islamic principles.

How do songs, music, and dance pose a threat to Taqwa and Allah consciousness among Muslims?

Songs, music, and dance often contain explicit or suggestive content that can lead individuals away from Taqwa and towards sinful behavior.

Why is it important for Muslims to recognize their responsibility in preserving Taqwa when attending or organizing parties?

Muslims are accountable for their actions and must uphold Taqwa even in social settings, ensuring they do not engage in activities that contradict Islamic values.

What are some common themes found in songs and music that can erode Taqwa and lead Muslims astray?

Songs and music often promote materialism, hedonism, and illicit relationships, all of which undermine the principles of Taqwa and Allah consciousness.

How does participation in dance, particularly with opposite sexes, compromise Taqwa and Islamic morals?

Dance movements, especially those with sexual connotations, encourage immodesty and inappropriate interactions that contradict the principles of Taqwa and modesty in Islam.

What steps can Muslims take to resist the temptation of participating in activities that undermine Taqwa, such as dance parties?

Muslims can prioritize their faith over worldly desires, avoid environments where their Taqwa may be compromised, and seek halal forms of entertainment.

Why is it important for Muslims to be discerning about the type of music they listen to and the messages it conveys?

Listening to music with inappropriate or immoral content can desensitize individuals to sin and weaken their Taqwa, leading them away from Allah's guidance.

How can Muslims maintain their Taqwa in environments where songs, music, and dance are prevalent, such as social gatherings or public events?

Muslims can adhere to Islamic principles of modesty, avoid situations that may tempt them to compromise their Taqwa, and surround themselves with like-minded individuals who prioritize Allah consciousness.

What role does self-discipline play in preserving Taqwa in the face of societal pressures to conform to secular norms?

Self-discipline allows Muslims to resist the allure of sinful activities, prioritize obedience to Allah's commandments, and maintain their Taqwa despite external influences.

How can parents and community leaders educate young Muslims about the importance of preserving Taqwa in all aspects of life, including entertainment choices?

Parents and community leaders can provide guidance on selecting appropriate forms of entertainment, instill a sense of accountability to Allah, and lead by example in upholding Taqwa.

What are some practical strategies for Muslims to strengthen their Taqwa and resist the temptation of indulging in sinful activities promoted by songs, music, and dance?

Engaging in regular acts of worship, seeking knowledge from authentic Islamic sources, and fostering a strong connection with Allah through remembrance and supplication.

How does peer pressure influence Muslims' decisions regarding participation in activities that may compromise their Taqwa?

Peer pressure can lead Muslims to prioritize social acceptance over adherence to Islamic principles, making it crucial for individuals to choose companions who encourage righteousness and Taqwa.

In what ways can Muslims use their creativity and talents to promote entertainment that aligns with Islamic values and preserves Taqwa?

Muslims can produce and support forms of entertainment, such as nasheeds and Islamic art, that inspire piety, virtue, and remembrance of Allah while avoiding the pitfalls of secular entertainment.

What are the spiritual and psychological benefits of prioritizing Taqwa over

temporary worldly pleasures offered by songs, music, and dance?

Prioritizing Taqwa brings inner peace, contentment, and closeness to Allah, while indulging in worldly pleasures may lead to guilt, emptiness, and spiritual distance.

How can Muslims strike a balance between enjoying permissible forms of entertainment and preserving their Taqwa in today's secularized society?

Muslims can seek entertainment that aligns with Islamic values, exercise moderation in their choices, and constantly evaluate whether their activities uphold their Taqwa and consciousness of Allah.

Why should Muslims prioritize their relationship with Allah over fleeting enjoyment derived from secular entertainment?

Prioritizing Allah's pleasure leads to lasting fulfillment and success in both this life and the Hereafter, whereas worldly pleasures offer only temporary satisfaction at the expense of Taqwa.

What are the consequences of neglecting Taqwa and indulging in activities that compromise one's faith and relationship with Allah?

Neglecting Taqwa can lead to spiritual decline, distance from Allah, and eventual regret and accountability on the Day of Judgment.

How can Muslim communities support individuals who are struggling to maintain their Taqwa in the face of societal pressures and temptations?

Muslim communities can offer guidance, support, and resources for individuals seeking to strengthen their Taqwa, creating an environment conducive to spiritual growth and adherence to Islamic principles.

For more information visit Quranexplains.com or contact Sheikh Touqeer Ansari.

"Impact of Songs, Music, and Dance on Tawheed and Taqwa Among Muslim Youth"

How do songs, music, and dance act as mediums for promoting behaviors that contradict Tawheed and Taqwa among Muslim youth?

These forms of entertainment often glorify worldly pleasures and indulgence, steering youth away from the principles of Tawheed and Taqwa.

Can you elaborate on how certain lyrics in songs or themes in music videos may undermine the belief in Tawheed among Muslim youth?

Lyrics and imagery in songs or music videos may promote materialism, idolization, or moral relativism, diluting the importance of Tawheed in the minds of youth.

What role does the rhythmic and emotive nature of music and dance play in captivating the hearts and minds of Muslim youth, potentially diverting them from the remembrance of Allah and the principles of Taqwa?

Music and dance have a powerful emotional impact, often leading youth to prioritize worldly pleasures over spiritual pursuits, thereby weakening their adherence to Taqwa.

How can exposure to songs, music, and dance in social settings contribute to desensitizing Muslim youth to behaviors that go against the teachings of Tawheed and Taqwa?

Regular exposure to such entertainment in social settings can desensitize youth to behaviors like immodesty, promiscuity, or materialism, gradually eroding their commitment to Tawheed and Taqwa.

Can you discuss how the normalization of certain behaviors in popular songs and music videos may lead Muslim youth to compromise their values associated with Tawheed and Taqwa?

When behaviors contrary to Islamic values are normalized in popular culture, Muslim youth may feel pressure to conform, thereby compromising their commitment to Tawheed and Taqwa.

What impact does the portrayal of relationships, romance, and physical attraction in songs, music, and dance have on the understanding of chastity and modesty among Muslim youth?

The glamorization of romantic relationships and physical attraction in these mediums may distort the perception of chastity and modesty, leading youth away from the principles of Tawheed and Taqwa.

How do music and dance events often serve as environments conducive to behaviors like mixing of genders, immodest attire, and consumption of prohibited substances, thereby weakening the practice of Taqwa among Muslim youth?

Music and dance events frequently encourage behaviors that violate Islamic principles of modesty, gender segregation, and substance avoidance, undermining the practice of Taqwa among youth.

Can you explain how the obsession with celebrity culture and fame perpetuated by songs, music, and dance may distract Muslim youth from the pursuit of spiritual growth associated with Tawheed and Taqwa?

The emphasis on celebrity culture and fame in these mediums may lead youth to prioritize worldly recognition over spiritual fulfillment, diverting their attention from Tawheed and Taqwa.

In what ways can the consumption of music and dance content through digital platforms and social media contribute to

the erosion of Tawheed and Taqwa among Muslim youth?

The easy accessibility of music and dance content on digital platforms and social media exposes youth to influences that undermine Tawheed and Taqwa, potentially leading them astray.

How does the participation in music and dance performances, whether in school settings or public events, sometimes lead Muslim youth to compromise their values rooted in Tawheed and Taqwa?

Participating in music and dance performances may require youth to engage in activities that conflict with Islamic values, creating internal conflicts regarding their adherence to Tawheed and Taqwa.

What role do parental guidance and community support play in helping Muslim youth navigate the influence of songs, music, and dance while upholding their commitment to Tawheed and Taqwa?

Strong parental guidance and community support can provide youth with the necessary guidance and resources to resist the negative influences of songs, music, and dance, reinforcing their commitment to Tawheed and Taqwa.

How can Islamic educational programs and initiatives incorporate discussions about the impact of songs, music, and dance on Tawheed and Taqwa to raise awareness among Muslim youth?

By addressing the influence of songs, music, and dance on Tawheed and Taqwa in educational settings, programs can empower youth to critically analyze media content and make choices aligned with their Islamic values.

What strategies can Muslim youth employ to minimize their exposure to songs, music, and dance content that may compromise their commitment to Tawheed and Taqwa?

Muslim youth can actively choose to avoid environments and media content that promote behaviors contrary to Tawheed and Taqwa, seeking alternative forms of entertainment and socialization that align with their values.

For more information visit Quranexplains.com or contact Sheikh Touqeer Ansari.

Preserving Tawheed: Safeguarding Against the Erosion of Faith

Tawheed, the fundamental belief in the oneness of Allah, stands as the cornerstone of Islamic faith and practice. In a world inundated with distractions and temptations, safeguarding Tawheed becomes paramount for Muslims seeking to uphold their spiritual integrity and resist the allure of societal norms that contradict Islamic principles.

In contemporary Western society, where indulgence in promiscuity, music, dance, and materialism often takes precedence, the essence of Tawheed is at risk of being diluted or even destroyed. The importance of Tawheed lies not only in its theological significance but also in its practical implications for navigating the moral challenges of modern life.

At its core, Tawheed emphasizes the exclusive worship and obedience to Allah alone, rejecting the worship of any other entities or desires. This concept serves as a safeguard against falling into the trap of associating partners with Allah, a grievous sin known as shirk. When individuals prioritize their own desires over the commandments of Allah, they inadvertently elevate their whims to the status of deities, thus violating the principle of Tawheed.

In the context of Western society, the erosion of Tawheed manifests in various forms, including the normalization of behaviors and practices that contradict Islamic teachings. From the glorification of material wealth to the promotion of hedonistic lifestyles, modern culture often encourages indulgence in activities that undermine the tenets of Tawheed.

Moreover, the pervasive influence of media, entertainment, and peer pressure further exacerbates the challenges faced by Muslims striving to uphold Tawheed. Music, movies, and social media platforms inundate individuals with messages that glorify worldly pleasures and promote self-gratification at the expense of spiritual fulfillment.

To counteract these influences and preserve Tawheed in the face of societal pressures, Muslims must remain steadfast in their commitment to Allah and His commandments. This requires a conscious effort to cultivate Taqwa, or God-consciousness, and prioritize obedience to Allah above all else. By aligning their actions with the teachings of Islam and seeking refuge in the remembrance of Allah, believers can shield themselves from the pitfalls of shirk and uphold the sanctity of Tawheed.

Furthermore, fostering a strong sense of community and seeking knowledge from reputable Islamic scholars can provide much-needed support and guidance in navigating the complexities of modern society while remaining true to the principles of Tawheed.

In essence, the preservation of Tawheed is not merely a theological concept but a practical imperative for Muslims striving to lead righteous lives amidst the moral challenges of contemporary Western society. By remaining vigilant against the erosion of faith and steadfast in their devotion to Allah, believers can safeguard the essence of Tawheed and uphold the purity of their faith.

Taqwa: Safeguarding Against Agnosticism and the Temptations of Music, Dance, and Entertainment

In the labyrinth of modernity, where the siren call of worldly pleasures beckons incessantly, Taqwa emerges as the steadfast anchor for believers navigating the tumultuous seas of faith. Taqwa, often translated as God-consciousness or piety, serves as a potent antidote to the creeping shadows of doubt and disbelief, particularly in the face of the seductive allure of music, dance, and entertainment. In this article, we explore the profound significance of Taqwa as a shield against agnosticism and the insidious influence of worldly temptations.

At its essence, Taqwa embodies a profound awareness of Allah's presence and an unwavering commitment to righteousness. It is the vigilant guard stationed at the gates of the heart, repelling the encroachment of doubt and disbelief with the radiant light of faith. Through Taqwa, believers cultivate a deep reverence for Allah and strive to align their actions with His divine commandments, thereby fortifying their spiritual fortress against the assaults of skepticism and uncertainty.

In the modern age, where agnosticism and atheism cast their long shadows over the landscape of faith, Taqwa emerges as the beacon of guidance illuminating the path of the believer. While agnosticism professes uncertainty regarding the existence of God, Taqwa instills in the believer an unshakeable conviction in the divine reality, rooted in contemplation, reflection, and unwavering trust in Allah's wisdom and mercy.

Furthermore, Taqwa serves as a safeguard against the pernicious influence of music, dance, and entertainment, which often serve as conduits for spiritual erosion and moral decay. In a world where hedonism reigns supreme and instant gratification is the order of the day, believers must exercise caution in their engagement with such temptations, lest they become ensnared in the web of sin and heedlessness.

Music, with its mesmerizing melodies and rhythmic beats, has the power to captivate the soul and stir the emotions. However, when devoid of spiritual content and moral guidance, it can lead the heart astray, dulling its sensitivity to the remembrance of Allah and paving the way for spiritual desolation. Similarly, dance and entertainment, while seemingly harmless forms of recreation, can subtly erode the barriers of Taqwa and undermine the believer's resolve in upholding righteous conduct.

In the face of these challenges, Taqwa emerges as the impregnable fortress of the believer, shielding them against the onslaught of temptation and moral decay. By cultivating a vigilant awareness of Allah's presence and a steadfast commitment to His commandments, believers fortify their hearts against the whispers of Shaytan and the allure of worldly pleasures.

In conclusion, Taqwa stands as the antidote to agnosticism and the temptations of music, dance, and entertainment, offering believers a pathway to spiritual fulfillment and moral integrity. By nurturing Taqwa in their hearts and minds, believers safeguard their faith against the corrosive influences of doubt and disbelief, emerging triumphant in their journey towards eternal salvation and divine pleasure.

The Armor of Tawheed: Fortifying Against Satanic Whispers and Spiritual Erosion

In the tumultuous journey of life, where the winds of temptation and doubt blow incessantly, the steadfast believer seeks refuge in the stronghold of Tawheed. Tawheed, the belief in the oneness of Allah, serves as a robust armor against the insidious whispers of Satan and the erosion of spiritual resolve. In this article, we delve into the profound significance of Tawheed as the ultimate defense mechanism in the face of adversity and spiritual decay.

At its core, Tawheed stands as the bedrock of Islamic faith, encapsulating the belief in the absolute oneness of Allah. It is the recognition that there is no deity worthy of worship except Allah, the Creator, Sustainer, and Sovereign of the universe. This profound acknowledgment forms the cornerstone of a believer's worldview, anchoring their faith in the divine unity and transcending the allure of false idols and worldly distractions.

One of the most potent effects of Tawheed is its ability to fortify the believer against Satanic whispers and doubts. Satan, the avowed adversary of humanity, ceaselessly endeavors to sow seeds of disbelief and discord in the hearts of believers. However, those firmly rooted in Tawheed remain impervious to his machinations, their unwavering faith serving as an impenetrable barrier against his deceitful stratagems.

The armor of Tawheed not only shields the believer from external threats but also bolsters their spiritual resilience from within. By recognizing the absolute sovereignty of Allah and entrusting their affairs to His divine wisdom, believers cultivate a profound sense of trust and contentment in the face of adversity. This unwavering reliance on Allah's will serves as a source of inner strength, enabling believers to navigate life's trials with patience and steadfastness.

Moreover, Tawheed serves as a beacon of guidance in the midst of moral ambiguity and spiritual erosion. In an age where societal norms and moral values are constantly challenged, the believer finds solace in the timeless truths of Tawheed. It instills in them a sense of moral clarity and purpose, enabling them to distinguish right from wrong and uphold the principles of righteousness and justice.

However, despite the inherent resilience of Tawheed, believers must remain vigilant against the subtle erosion of faith caused by the enticements of the world. In an era characterized by materialism, hedonism, and moral relativism, the believer must be discerning in guarding their hearts against the corrosive influences of sin and temptation. The allure of worldly pleasures, be it in the form of song, music, or dance, can gradually erode the fortress of Tawheed if left unchecked.

Therefore, it is incumbent upon believers to strengthen their resolve in Tawheed through steadfast adherence to Islamic teachings and practices. Regular remembrance of Allah, diligent study of the Quran, and sincere supplication serve as potent weapons in the arsenal of the believer, fortifying their faith and safeguarding them against spiritual erosion.

In conclusion, Tawheed stands as the impregnable fortress of the believer, shielding them against the onslaught of Satanic whispers and the erosion of spiritual resolve. By embracing the profound truth of Tawheed and embodying its principles in their lives, believers fortify themselves against the vicissitudes of life and emerge triumphant in their journey towards spiritual fulfillment and eternal salvation.

Defending Faith: The Role of Tawheed in Combatting Atheism and Taqwa as the Shield Against the Temptations of Music, Dance, and Entertainment

In the ever-evolving landscape of faith and belief systems, the concept of Tawheed stands as an indomitable fortress, guarding the hearts and minds of believers against the onslaught of atheism and doubt. Tawheed, the belief in the oneness of Allah, serves as the bedrock of Islamic theology, providing a robust framework for understanding the divine and navigating the complexities of the world. In this article, we delve into the pivotal role of Tawheed in combatting atheism and explore how Taqwa serves as the shield against the allure of music, dance, and entertainment, safeguarding the faith of Muslims.

At its core, Tawheed asserts the absolute unity and sovereignty of Allah, affirming His oneness in His essence, attributes, and actions. This fundamental tenet of Islamic belief serves as the cornerstone upon which the entire edifice of faith is erected, offering believers a clear and unambiguous understanding of the divine reality. In a world where atheism seeks to undermine the existence of God through skepticism and rational inquiry, Tawheed stands as the impregnable fortress, repelling the assaults of doubt and disbelief with the irrefutable truth of divine unity.

Moreover, Tawheed serves as a beacon of guidance, illuminating the path of believers and empowering them to withstand the allure of atheistic ideologies. By affirming the oneness of Allah and acknowledging His sovereignty over all creation, believers find solace and reassurance in the knowledge that their faith is grounded in divine truth, transcending the limitations of human understanding and intellectual inquiry.

In addition to Tawheed, Taqwa emerges as the shield against the temptations of music, dance, and entertainment, which often serve as conduits for moral decay and spiritual erosion. Taqwa, often translated as God-consciousness or piety, instills in believers a profound awareness of Allah's presence and a steadfast commitment to righteousness. It serves as the vigilant guard stationed at the gates of the heart, repelling the encroachment of sin and heedlessness with the radiant light of faith.

In a world saturated with sensory stimuli and hedonistic pleasures, Taqwa reminds believers of their ultimate purpose in life and guides them towards righteousness and moral integrity. By cultivating Taqwa in their hearts and minds, believers fortify themselves against the corrosive influences of music, dance, and entertainment, which often lead to spiritual desolation and moral decay.

In conclusion, Tawheed and Taqwa emerge as the twin pillars of faith, defending believers against the onslaught of atheism and the temptations of worldly pleasures. By upholding the principles of Tawheed and cultivating Taqwa in their hearts and minds, Muslims can fortify their faith and emerge triumphant in the face of adversity, steadfast in their commitment to the worship of Allah alone and the pursuit of righteousness.

The Universal Quest: Understanding Our Creator, Allah, Beyond Religion

In the vast tapestry of human existence, lies a fundamental quest that transcends the boundaries of religion: the quest to understand our Creator, Allah. Regardless of one's religious affiliation, the pursuit of knowledge about the divine essence that underpins all of existence is a responsibility incumbent upon every human being.

This pursuit begins with an acknowledgment of the undeniable truth that there exists a Creator, a Supreme Being who is the source of all existence. Regardless of the name by which we address Him, whether it be Allah, God, or any other, the essence remains the same: an omnipotent, omniscient Creator who is the ultimate source of everything in the universe.

To embark on this journey of understanding, one must open their hearts and minds to the vast repository of knowledge available through scientific research, technological advancements, and spiritual exploration. It is through this multidimensional approach that we can begin to unravel the mysteries of our existence and gain insight into the nature of our Creator.

Scientific research and technological advancements offer us glimpses into the intricate workings of the universe, allowing us to marvel at the complexity and order that pervades every aspect of creation. From the microscopic realm of subatomic particles to the cosmic expanse of galaxies and nebulae, each discovery serves as a testament to the sublime wisdom and power of our Creator.

Yet, our quest for understanding goes beyond the confines of empirical observation and rational inquiry. It extends into the realm of spiritual exploration, where the heart seeks communion with the divine through prayer, contemplation, and introspection. It is in the stillness of the soul that we may perceive the subtle whispers of our Creator, guiding us towards a deeper understanding of His infinite mercy and compassion.

Central to this quest for understanding is the recognition of Allah as the sustainer and caretaker of all that exists. From the majestic mountains to the smallest insect, from the depths of the oceans to the vastness of space, every creature and every phenomenon bears the imprint of His divine providence. It is this realization that instills within us a sense of awe and reverence for the majesty of our Creator, inspiring us to seek His guidance and grace in all aspects of our lives.

In conclusion, the quest to understand our Creator, Allah, is a universal endeavor that transcends the boundaries of religion. It is a journey of discovery and enlightenment that beckons to all humanity, inviting us to delve deeper into the mysteries of existence and forge a deeper connection with the divine. By embracing the multidimensional nature of this quest, we can enrich our lives with a profound sense of purpose, meaning, and fulfillment, drawing ever closer to the ultimate truth that lies at the heart of all creation.

Last Words

Here's an explanation of some of the most important issues for Muslims living in Western societies, especially for their future generations who are born and raised there:

Understanding of Taqwa and Tawheed: Taqwa refers to God-consciousness or piety, while Tawheed is the concept of the Oneness of Allah. These are fundamental principles of Islamic belief and practice. Muslims in Western societies often face challenges in fully understanding and internalizing these concepts due to cultural differences and language barriers. Providing accessible resources, such as those available on Quranexplains.com, can help bridge this gap and enable Western Muslims to deepen their understanding of Taqwa and Tawheed.

Differentiating Atheism and Agnosticism: Atheism is the lack of belief in any gods or deities, while agnosticism is the view that the existence of God is unknown or unknowable. Many Muslims living in Western societies may encounter atheistic or agnostic viewpoints, which can pose challenges to their faith. Educating them about the differences between atheism, agnosticism, and Islamic beliefs can help them navigate these challenges and strengthen their faith.

Access to Islamic Education and Resources: Providing English literature on Islamic teachings is crucial for Muslims in Western societies, especially for the younger generation. Accessible resources, such as books, websites, and educational materials, can help them learn about their faith in a language and format that resonates with their cultural background and upbringing. Supporting initiatives to create and distribute English literature on Islamic teachings, as advocated by Quranexplains.com, can empower Western Muslims to enrich their knowledge and understanding of Islam.

Supporting Masjids and Islamic Centers: Masjids and Islamic centers play a vital role in the Muslim community, serving as places of worship, education, and community engagement. Supporting initiatives to provide English literature and resources for masjids can help strengthen the Muslim community in Western societies and ensure that future generations have access to Islamic education and guidance.

Cultivating a Vibrant Muslim Identity: Muslims in Western societies often grapple with questions of identity and belonging. Empowering them with knowledge about their faith, heritage, and cultural values can help cultivate a vibrant and thriving Muslim identity. Encouraging engagement with Islamic teachings and community activities can foster a sense of belonging and connection among Western Muslims, especially for the younger generation growing up in diverse and multicultural societies.

In summary, addressing issues such as understanding Taqwa and Tawheed, differentiating atheism and agnosticism, providing access to Islamic education and resources, supporting masjids and Islamic centers, and cultivating a vibrant Muslim identity are essential for Muslims living in Western societies, particularly for their future generations. Initiatives like Quranexplains.com that focus on providing English literature on Islamic teachings play a crucial role in addressing these issues and empowering Western Muslims to navigate their faith in a multicultural and diverse environment.

Send your donations and Zakat for most important cause
ansari.touqeer.toronto@gmail.com